IN THE NAME OF GOD

Entrepreneurship as done by

Yousef Sedighi

The Founder of
Yahya Shoe company

Written by:
Dr. Reza Yadegari
Dr. Mahshid Sanaeefard
The Winners of the Prestigious
Jalal Al-e Ahmad Literary Award
and
Aryaan Yadegari
Lilyaan Yadegari
The Second Generation Authors of the
Great Iranian Entrepreneur Book Collection

Serial Number: P2446190215
Title: Entrepreneurship as done by Yousef Sedighi
Subtitle: The Founder of Yahya Shoe Company
Authors: Dr. Reza Yadegari & Dr. Mahshid Sanaeefard
Co-Authors: Aryaan Yadegari & Lilyaan Yadegari
ISBN: 978-1-77892-140-7
Metadata: Biography & Entrepreneurship
Book Size: Paperback
Pages: 62
Canada Publish Date: September 2024
Publisher: Kidsocado Publishing House

Copyright @ 2024 By Kidsocado Publishing House
All Rights Reserved, including the right of production in whole or in part in any form.

Kidsocado Publishing house
Vancouver, Canada

Phone: +1 (833) 633 8654
WhatsApp: +1 (236) 333 7248
Email: info@kidsocado.com
https://kidsocado.com

- **Introduction** 3
- **The Greenlight** 5
- **The life and world of Yousef Sedighi** 7
- **The analysis of the founder of Yahya Shoe company** 67

Introduction

The work of identifying the greatest Iranian entrepreneurs got underway back in 1997 with the help and assistance of my wife Dr. Mahshid Sanaeefard, the Manager of the Great Iranian Entrepreneurs Publication. An exceptionally long and arduous task, which has enabled us to gain substantial insight into the world of entrepreneurship and job creation, and thus make history for the future generation of Iranians by helping found and chart a whole new path towards true success in business and industry alike.

Next to winning numerous international awards on this incredible journey of countless ups and downs, we have cooperated and collaborated extensively with some of Iran's highly accredited and most reputable higher learning centers, like Sharif Industrial University, University of Science and Technology, Alzahra University and Shahid Beheshti University. Moreover, we have also successfully established and registered the International Qualification and Certification Auditors Company or IQCA in Canada, whose main role and responsibility is to publish the life history of the greatest Iranian entrepreneurs to make them known by name to the other people in the world. IQCA has also been highly active in setting up and establishing an award presentation scheme in Iran in order to identify and introduce the country's most creative individuals and organizations, and thereby aid and assist with promoting them on a global scale.

It is hoped that as a special and leading group, we are able to introduce the most powerful Iranian women and me to the rest of the world and at the same time, identify and retell the life stories of the best role models for Iran's next generation.

Dr. Reza Yadegari
www.UNESCO.ws

The Greenlight

The movement to transfer the experiences of the world's greatest entrepreneurs is one of the most important factors in helping the American and European companies and organizations' progress and improvement. These companies and organizations had concluded rather smartly that if a society wishes significant advancement and development, it must keep its eye on the experiences of the previous generation and not allow the young to incur costs on the system by experiencing and learning through trial and error. In line with the same notion, entrepreneurship has the potential to create notable transformation throughout a given society's various levels provided it is implemented using principles and plans that take advantage of the experiences of the proficient and skilled members. Allowing the young to take over across the world is certainly a commendable measure, which has also been taken in our beloved Iran as well, except that here the experiences of the previous generation of entrepreneurs and managers has never been made properly available for application by the new generation – something that has regrettably inflicted irrecoverable costs onto the country because of the continuous repetition of the same old mistakes. Our project to identify the greatest Iranian entrepreneurs, so that we may research their lives to understand the reasons and factors for their success started off back in 1997 simultaneously as the arrival of the novel science of entrepreneurship in Iran. Admittedly, the path has been a long one involving strenuous effort. In the years following the events of the Iranian Revolution, literary no entrepreneur in the country was willing to unveil and reveal herself or himself and the experiences she or he possessed.

In spite of this, we were quite determined to fulfil our goal of teaching and training the future generation by documenting and publishing the life stories and experiences of Iran's greatest entrepreneurs through a one-thousand-volume book aptly titled 'Entrepreneurship as done by …' What is presented in the book collection, is rare and valuable roadmap designed based on the experiences and performances of Iran's greatest economic minds, which undoubtedly can be a wonderful asset in guiding and directing anyone who intends to get involved in any type of commercial, production and service provision activity. We hope that our collection book can help open up doors and pave the way for Iran's new generation of young entrepreneurs, and also remain a lasting piece of literary work to remember us by.

Dr. Reza Yadegari
Dr. Mahshid Sanaeefard
Tehran, Iran 2021

The life and world of Yousef Sedighi

My Childhood

I, Yousef, was born in 1986 in the Tehranpars neighborhood of Tehran, becoming the second child in the Sedighi family. Although I had two brothers, my parents focused more on me, running alongside me from day one because I was a curious child who wanted to manage everything. I remember my mother teaching bead embroidery and flower making at home, and at the age of seven, I learned sewing techniques by watching her hands. Sometimes, when my mother was busy, I would teach her students, impressing everyone with my skill and insight. Leadership and management were innate in me, and from a young age, I wanted to take charge of everything and always took the initiative.

In middle school, my mother hired an English tutor for all three of us to ensure we became proficient in the language. The education system at the time was weak in teaching English, and most students finished high school without mastering the language. My mother always emphasized the importance of being fluent in English for career advancement. Despite being a mischievous child and my mother's strictness, I only learned English intermittently, often taking long breaks between lessons. It's worth noting that mastering English as a second language in Iran is challenging due to limited exposure and daily use, making it easy to forget without regular practice.

Alongside my studies, I began selling from an early age. I had a box of surprise toys and spent summers selling balloons and gum to neighborhood kids. At twelve, I stopped enjoying Tehran's summer fun as I started working as an apprentice at my father's shop in the market right after my exams. I learned from my father by observing his interactions with customers and gradually mastered the art of sales and customer relations.

The Bitter Tale of My Father

My father was originally in the business of selling safety equipment like gloves and workwear. My mother recounts that he was so dedicated to his work that he was five hours late for their wedding because he was securing an order for safety gloves! My father was a hardworking and disciplined man who never compromised on quality, a trait he learned from a young age when he was forced into the world of work at five.

Born into a poor family in a mountainous village in Ardabil, he lost both parents simultaneously at five, becoming an orphan. The villagers were too poor to take him in, so his uncle from Tehran took him under his wing and brought him to the city. His uncle was among the first to sell safety equipment in Iran. My father started working as his assistant at six and became so skilled that by eleven, he was traveling alone to Isfahan to manage his uncle's accounts and collect payments.

Despite the hardships and lack of support from others, my father persevered and, by his forties, had built a successful business, only to lose everything due to a business dispute.

The Nader Shoes Incident

Twenty years ago, when I was 16 or 17, a significant crisis hit our family. Although my father had a stake in a shop and was a partner with his uncle, competitors advised him to leave the safety equipment business and venture into the shoe industry. After much deliberation, my father decided to represent Nader Shoes. However, he struggled alone and couldn't manage everything by himself.

My mother, then thirty and managing the household and our education, decided to help him. Soon, my brothers and I joined in. At that time, I was in my pre-university year, with only weeks left before university entrance exams. I decided to drop out and work full-time with my father. Despite being the top student in my class, I chose to support my father because I didn't want him to face another failure.

I worked day and night for six months with my parents at Nader Shoes. As the sales systems became computerized, I spent most of my time setting up our sales system. After ensuring my parents were proficient in sales, I opened another branch in Haft Hoz, managing it alone. However, after eight months, I realized I was making no profit and could barely cover the rent. I decided to close the branch and used the deposit to buy a shop in Hassan Abad, set to open in three years.

Returning to the Safety Equipment Business

With no other options, I returned to my father's old trade and apprenticed for three years among seasoned safety and firefighting equipment sellers. My father, scarred by past business disputes, was reluctant about my return to this trade. But I was determined to master it and surpass everyone. Despite working under a colleague who was harsh on me, knowing my ambitions, I learned everything from him. I read product labels and used my English skills to understand their uses better than others.

My perseverance paid off, and after a few years of apprenticeship, I opened my own shop. I sourced safety equipment from a Taiwanese company and built a trusted relationship with a Dubai supplier, becoming their exclusive distributor in Iran. Over the next two years, I expanded my business and became a leading supplier of all types of safety equipment, outperforming my competitors.

Yahya Shoes

I became a distributor for two types of safety shoes, but due to quality issues with imports, I decided to start my own production. Knowing the importance of proper footwear for workers, I ensured all our shoes met high standards, regardless of price. By 2009, I decided to establish my own shoe factory. Despite never having seen a shoe factory, I was determined.

My journey from a curious child to a business leader has been marked by perseverance, learning, and a relentless drive to lead and innovate.

Starting my business was incredibly challenging. As some friends and acquaintances put it, I entered this industry with sheer determination and tackled each stage of establishment and production one step at a time. While training the factory workers, I was also learning myself, constantly updating my knowledge about safety shoe production. Because the factory was located in a deprived area in the south of the city, I had to oversee everything meticulously.

For example, there were times when I hired workers who had more sewing expertise than I did. Over time, their confidence would grow to the point where they would challenge my authority and form their own factions among the workers. I had to manage these situations tactfully, ensuring that all the unruly workers became compliant. I had to experiment with every possible method to succeed and stay on this path.

Once, my factory was shut down because we had copied the sole of a European shoe. Another individual had registered the sole design under his name and sued us. It took two years in court to prove that the sole had a foreign origin and that our intention was to prevent workers from slipping and getting injured, which is why we didn't alter the original design. This legal battle taught me to approach every aspect of production with a professional and specialized mindset.

As a result, I decided to hire the best specialists in shoe production for my factory. We began our operations not only scientifically and academically but also by focusing on three fundamental principles:
1. Maslow's Hierarchy of Needs
2. Psychology emphasizing reason, memory, will, imagination, and nature
3. Persian Translation of the Quran

Combining these three crucial elements, I developed the factory's rules and the unique management style of Yousef Sedighi.

The Name Yahya

At twenty-three, I got married, and two years later, when my wife became pregnant, we chose the name Yahya for our son from among the blessed names in the Quran. Since my son's birth and the establishment of the shoe factory happened simultaneously, I decided to name our product line after Yahya. This choice was not random or without reason.

Since I can remember, I have read the Quran countless times, especially in Persian, always trying to analyze the meanings of the verses. Before Yahya's birth, while reading Surah Maryam, I came across these verses:

"In the name of God, the Most Gracious, the Most Merciful. This is a reminder of God's blessing upon His servant, Zechariah. At the time when he prayed in his sanctuary, he said: "O Lord, old age has overtaken me, and my bones have become weak. Furthermore, my wife is barren and unable to conceive.

Grant me a child from Your bounty, one who is pleasing to You, for I fear that after my death, my people will not be able to uphold the traditions of Abraham and Jacob."

And in the following verse, God responds: "O Zechariah, indeed We give you good tidings of a boy whose name will be Yahya. We have not assigned to any before this name."

From these verses, I realized that Yahya is the only name directly given by God. The name Yahya, which is parallel to the name Azrael but in contrast to it—because Azrael takes life, whereas Yahya means 'giver of life'—captivated me. After consulting with my wife, we decided to name our precious son Yahya.

The name Yahya derives from "Hayy," meaning life. Additionally, Yahya aligns with the Hebrew name for God, "Yahweh," the oldest known name for God on earth, meaning "I am who I am." In Judaism, "Yahweh" is one of the forbidden names that cannot be given to a person.

When the shoe factory started, we couldn't find a more fitting name for our products. The name Yahya brought many blessings to our work. What greater miracle could happen in my life than having the only blessed name given by God as part of me, allowing me to honor God's name by producing quality products?

I draw much inspiration from the Quran and its revelations in my life, and I have an unwavering trust in God and the extraordinary things He has done in my life.

I believe strongly in cause and effect, and I conduct my work based on mathematical logic and rational reasoning. For instance, if I instruct my team to perform a task, I have already prepared twenty reasons and justifications for issuing that order.

Yahya's Factory Rules

• In our factory, like in Japan, there is no wastage of human resources.
• Mischief and playfulness have no place because we have sealed off all avenues for such behavior.
• Despite having a large workforce, our efficiency and profit margins are high because we have always focused on entrepreneurship and creating new opportunities from day one.
• Our workers must continually increase their knowledge and stay updated with current information.
• Mental health, trustworthiness, and adaptability are more important to us than physical health and teamwork.

I teach these rules to my employees during work and encourage them to elevate their positions. Unfortunately, many Iranians tend to progress well initially but then regress, similar to an hourglass. For example, a renowned barber might struggle to expand his business despite his initial success. I believe that entrepreneurship requires specific knowledge and should be driven by specialists in the field.

Moreover, I think that success depends on one's curiosity. For instance, if I take an employee to a horse-riding club ten times, they might never ask about horses or riding. In contrast, my nature is very inquisitive. If I visit a pharmaceutical workshop, I will ask thirty questions in the first session and three hundred in the second. This curiosity is essential because "the bane of knowledge is the illusion of knowing." Knowledge is an endless ocean, and the more one learns, the more one realizes how little they know.

Our Training Process
1. Recognition
2. Change in Performance
3. Ability
4. Skill

A crucial lesson I've learned from Japanese work methods is that they continue training workers until they reach a level of skill. In other countries, training often stops once a worker is deemed capable. This principle also applies to raising my son, Yahya. Today, both Yahya and Yahya's Shoe Factory are ten years old, and soon, Yahya will need to manage the factory. Therefore, I strive to equip him with the highest management skills. I let him occasionally purchase items like pens or band-aids and sell them to the workers. I believe that those who want to enter the world of business should understand commerce from childhood, practicing negotiation and customer attraction. Contrary to many parents who want to shield their children from the hardships they faced, I want my son to experience those challenges but, in a manner, aligned with his interests and within ethical boundaries.

Five Essential Principles of Yahya's Factory

As mentioned earlier, we once had to close our factory, which turned out to be beneficial. This closure revealed many issues, such as recognizing that some problems were due to employee mischief aimed at harming our business. This experience helped me understand my environment better and resolve to base my work on current knowledge and expertise.

From my perspective, there are five essential principles, or "MS," for establishing a successful business:

1. Intelligence: Ensure that employees have sufficient knowledge for their roles, acknowledging that no one can claim to have complete intelligence.
2. Memory
3. Willpower
4. Imagination: Useful for finding creative solutions to obstacles.
5. Character: Employees must have integrity, avoid lying, deceit, and jealousy.

I consider these five principles when hiring, and if someone lacks them, they have no place in our factory.

Qualities of an Employer

An aspiring entrepreneur and manager must assess themselves against these eight criteria:

1. Can they gather and lead people?
2. Can they motivate their workers?
3. Can they place the right people in the right positions?
4. Can they form a cohesive administrative team, similar to an architect ensuring resources and labor are available before con-

struction?

5. Are they confident in their work methods?

6. Can they obtain proper planning from their managers?

7. Do they know how to read reports?

8. Can they ensure access to all necessary materials for their product, akin to a chef ensuring all ingredients are available before cooking?

Anyone who can confidently affirm their ability in these eight areas can start their work on a small scale with minimal staff. Start with small tasks and gradually move on to bigger ones. For instance, someone wanting to start a shoe factory should begin with a small workshop and focus on producing one type of product. Start with making slippers, then gradually move into the shoe manufacturing industry in a specialized manner.

Evaluate yourself to see if you can interact with different types of people. Everyone has different temperaments and attitudes. Some people are defensive toward the employer's demands, while others are exhausting to deal with. Assess if you can choose the right personnel. How do you react if a worker makes a mistake? Do you lose your temper and treat everyone the same, causing them to leave, or can you manage the problem effectively?

Human resource management is critical and sensitive in this field. I personally visit the factory three times a week to ensure everyone is in their proper place and no one is mistakenly occupying someone else's role. Since both men and women work in the same space, there's no room for oglers in our organization.

Three employees are dedicated to monitoring and behavioral analysis. Mental health and sanity among workers are paramount to me.

High-Quality Production

We started Yahya's Factory with a premium product. Safety shoes come in weak, average, and good quality levels. We began with high-quality, top-tier shoes. We chose one model and focused on producing that model with the best quality. We didn't diversify too much in models because I believe that over-diversification is a weakness among our competitors. They often take a month to fulfill orders because they are producing various models and colors. From the start, we announced that we would produce limited models in bulk and keep our warehouses stocked. This approach has been one of Yahya Shoes' success factors. When we receive an order for six thousand pairs today, the order is ready by the next morning because our warehouse is always full.

From day one, we focused on producing high-quality products rather than playing with models. We realized that mediocre products are widely produced, so we aimed to introduce our brand with superior quality. I named the brand Yahya, so I was meticulous about quality control, ensuring no mistakes were made.

Currently, around 40 employees in the factory are dedicated solely to quality control and oversight. At least five quality control inspectors are stationed in each hall, meticulously evaluating all aspects. Since we produce shoes for workers, our primary focus is on quality and worker comfort. Unfortunately, some contractors don't care about workers' mental health, only providing safety gear during inspections to meet contractual obligations. However, many large, reputable companies have welcomed Yahya Safety Shoes, and my relatives, who entered the safety equipment industry through my uncle, can best guarantee the safety of our products.

Face Mask Production During COVID-19

We started producing Yahya Shoes in 2013, and by 2019, when the COVID-19 pandemic hit, we had grown significantly. Before the virus was officially declared a pandemic by government agencies, I saw a chart online comparing the spread rates of SARS, Ebola, and COVID-19. Using my mathematical mind and strong reasoning, I calculated and informed those around me that COVID-19 would soon reach Iran. We needed to prepare strong masks for our employees. There was no time to buy a mask production machine, so I designed a human-powered machine based on a German mask-making machine model. Germans, due to high labor costs, design machines to minimize human involvement, while in Iran, we prefer using human labor due to high production costs.

I adapted the German machine model using the workers' arms to replace machine bearings. Our innovative machine was 85 times faster than the sample machine. Our process combined human labor and shoe-cutting machinery, stitching multilayered cuts together. After the Vice President, the Minister of Industry, and the Tehran Standard officials visited our factory and appreciated our initiative, the television showcased our workshop for a month.

We later added an autoclave to the process for thorough disinfection. All masks were placed in special autoclave bags and steam-sterilized at 125 degrees Fahrenheit, producing high-quality masks befitting human dignity. We pioneered fabric masks, which weren't available in other countries before. These masks lasted up to a year. Initially, we gifted 10,000 masks to gas station employees nationwide and sent masks to various large organizations. My primary concern was the health of my fellow citizens and preventing the virus's spread, not profitability.

Due to the pandemic, businesses were closed, and I feared liquidity issues. I sold my BMW X4 to cover the budget shortfall, as we had increased our workforce from 120 to 500 people. Most of the car sale proceeds were spent on purchasing fabric and elastic bands for masks and paying workers' wages.

Producing fabric masks had its challenges. Elastic bands and fabric were hard to find. Elastic prices skyrocketed overnight, forcing me to hire three motorcycle couriers to scour the city for supplies at any cost. Given the critical nature of public health, I couldn't focus on the cost of raw materials. It was essential to keep production going and ensure the well-being of my compatriots. Sometimes, due to unreliable suppliers, I had to buy fabric at exorbitant prices to ensure timely delivery to workers. My sole intention was to serve the people and save lives during these challenging times. Today, seeing so many people still using our masks fills me with pride for my dedicated and hardworking team. Many employees worked multiple shifts around the clock. For instance, some workers were tasked with sewing filters onto masks for bulk orders but struggled to keep up. Therefore, I added a night shift, bringing in two busloads of additional staff. As the day and evening shift supervisors grew tired, I took over as the night shift supervisor, personally training new and inexperienced workers. Volunteer police officers also joined us to maintain security. When work is done for God's satisfaction and people's well-being, all conditions align seamlessly, and divine blessings make everything possible. Producing masks brought us honor and respect from God, far more important than material gains.

An Unmatched Market

In Iran today, the production of safety shoes is minimal. For instance, there may be around 30 safety shoe manufacturers across the country, but 10 of them ceased operations last year due to bankruptcy. Those who dominated the market lost control due to long-term, one-year checks. In the current climate of rapid inflation, it is no longer feasible to produce goods on one-year credit terms. As a result, customers have stopped ordering from these manufacturers. Occasionally, some competitors offer products at lower prices, causing market instability. Now, with increased tax scrutiny, some competitors can no longer operate as before and attempt to advance their work with mobile checks.

However, the situation at Yahya Factory has improved compared to the past. We've doubled our production in the last three months, increased our workforce, and are in the process of opening a second branch in Ardabil.

Industrial Growth Model in Iran

In Iran, everything seems to go against global economic equations. For example, under current conditions, everyone agrees that manufacturing and running factories are not profitable. From my experience, this is primarily due to inflation, which is the biggest enemy of job creation and a major hindrance to production focus.

When I started producing Yahya shoes, I thought I could buy a bigger house for my family with the factory's profits by the end of the year. However, within a few months, property prices in this country multiplied, while our profits remained the same as last year.

Globally, if you buy a house with an area of 'n' this year, next year, due to depreciation and the aging of materials, you would have to sell it for 'n-1'. In contrast, in Iran, if you convert your capital into land or property, its value will increase at least fivefold in a few years. For instance, if I were to fire all my staff today, sell all the factory assets and property, and buy a large piece of land in a remote village with the proceeds, my capital would increase tenfold after ten years. In industrial work, our initial investment retains its value over 10-20 years, and sometimes, the product's value even decreases. Consequently, few investors are willing to venture into production and job creation. Until money circulates within the production cycle, the economic wheel of society will falter, and no one, not even the investor, will experience relative comfort and well-being.

Entrepreneurship and production require passion. If we focus solely on economic calculations, there is no profit, and the economic justification is unpredictable. Production and job creation demand a special passion, a need to define the societal demand for the product, and a thorough assessment of all aspects.

The Tehran Factory

In the past decade, we had to relocate the factory 5-6 times because the rented premises couldn't keep up with our rapid growth. Sometimes, we had to move twice in a single year to accommodate the increasing volume of orders. We needed to add more machines to increase production. During the 2019-2020 COVID-19 outbreak, we added more machines to produce fabric masks. By 2021, we were able to settle in a 500,000-square-meter factory, thanks to God's grace. As the COVID-19 situation eased and a large portion of the population got vaccinated, we scaled back mask production and set aside a few mask-producing machines in a corner of the factory.

A shoe factory owner must simultaneously focus on human resources and mechanical equipment. Therefore, shoe production is one of the hardest jobs in the world, comparable to constructing a building. Producing 20,000 pairs of shoes a day is akin to constructing 20,000 houses. I believe it is even more challenging than building construction because, in construction, there are specialists like supervising engineers and architects. In our factory, we don't have shoe supervisors or shoe architects; we have to train new hires from scratch. After completing their training, some become arrogant and want to work independently. In the shoe industry, skilled workers like cutters, leather workers, and injection workers are all highly specialized. Some, after learning all the skills, become arrogant and lose their genuine humility, wanting to break away. Some go to rival manufacturers and badmouth us to elevate their status in another factory. As a manager and entrepreneur, I must always be mindful of all the details and personalities within my team.

The Ardabil Factory

During the peak of COVID-19, we donated masks to various places, from Hassanabad Square in Tehran to gas stations nationwide and remote villages. We even sent free masks to villages around Ardabil, including my father's hometown. After some time, I had a meeting with the Imam of Ardabil, who had invited me to his office to express his gratitude. He said, "We have active young workers here in Ardabil who are mostly unemployed due to lack of investment and job creation. If you establish a business here, we will provide all the necessary support."

This prompted me to decide to establish the second branch of Yahya Shoes in Ardabil. After setting up the factory, I noticed significant differences between the workforce in Tehran and Ardabil. The most important difference is that workers in Ardabil do not become arrogant after training and, due to the lack of local competitors, do not seek to change their workplace after a short period. Their work pace and motivation to learn are higher than those of the workers in Tehran, consuming less energy and capital from us. However, it has its challenges. For instance, most workers are not organizational and require extensive training. Initially, the Imam Khomeini Relief Committee introduced some workers to us and even covered their insurance, but it still required more focus and follow-up.

Currently, there are 300 workers in the Tehran factory and about 70 skilled workers in Ardabil, with the number increasing.

To oversee the Ardabil factory, I had to leave my comfort zone in Tehran, and managing two branches simultaneously requires higher vigilance. However, I enjoy this busy and stressful work because I believe stress is essential for an entrepreneur as it keeps them alive and alert.

After establishing the Ardabil factory, I gained more respect and recognition among my colleagues and safety equipment vendors in Hassanabad. Most of the vendors and importers are originally from Ardabil and warmly welcomed the establishment of the second branch of Yahya Shoes in Ardabil.

Yahya's Food Initiative in Ardabil

After setting up the Yahya Shoes factory in Ardabil, I decided to open a sandwich shop specializing in hot dogs. From the start,

I told the operators that I wouldn't take any profit from it. We would work together, and any profit that came my way would be spent for charitable purposes. This sandwich shop initiated a chain of goodwill. My goal is to open another branch on the other side of the intersection in question. It is a charitable venture providing sandwiches at half the market price to customers and those in need. We agreed with the staff to distribute 50 free sandwiches for every 500 sold. We also send free sandwiches to many organizations like police stations and welfare centers. I plan to open branches of Yahya Sandwich across Iran in most cities. This business is very blessed, and as the Yahya brand becomes more recognized, our shoe customers also increase.

I believe that the stronger a person is, the less others will challenge or envy them. True friends become more apparent, and those wearing masks naturally drift away. Few people envy a successful entrepreneur's wealth because they see them as deserving of it. For example, if you see a large, luxurious villa in a resort area and learn that it belongs to a factory owner or entrepreneur, you feel happy and admire them. However, if you discover that a government official or parliament member owns it, you feel unhappy and complain because you know they didn't earn it through honest effort and hard work.

Similarly, you can't criticize the wealth of the owner of Mihan Ice Cream because you have been their customer since childhood, and their brand's success is the result of continuous effort and perseverance.

In Japan, from ministers to administrative staff, everyone strives to ensure that creative and entrepreneurial individuals succeed in their work. Societies have always relied on their creative and entrepreneurial forces. Since ancient times, while rulers and kings were preoccupied with defending their realms, creative and entrepreneurial individuals were providing food and necessities for the people under those rulers. It is the entrepreneurial and productive force that can prevent famine and bankruptcy in a society.

Today, I believe we should constantly honor entrepreneurs like those in the food industry, such as Bijan. Without the 2,000 trucks of Bijan Company, other producers would face exorbitant costs and food shortages. For example, Bijan distributes products from Rani Company. If Rani were to purchase trucks or hire agencies for distribution, their costs would be several times higher. However, through an agreement with Bijan, they store all their products in Bijan's warehouse, and Bijan distributes them nationwide for a 7% share of the sales. The economy of a society revolves around its entrepreneurs.

The Difference Between Producing Safety Shoes and Personal Shoes

In a forty-square-meter space, you can produce 100 pairs of personal shoes daily. Making personal or urban shoes is much easier than industrial shoes because personal shoes do not require injection molding. You might wonder, what is injection molding? When the shoe upper is ready, materials like hot tar are poured into a mold, which quickly descends and simultaneously bonds the sole to the upper. However, in 95% of personal shoes, the sole and the upper are made separately and then glued together.

At Yahya Shoes, our specialty is safety shoes, so we don't produce injected shoes. Instead, we use the press method to bond heated materials and then finish them. Most of our clients are large factories and petrochemical companies. For eight years, Khorasan Steel has exclusively sourced its workers' safety shoes from us. Before opening their factory, Behran Oil Company also partnered with us for safety equipment, and to this day, they procure all their safety gear and shoes from us. Since Yahya is now a recognized brand, we plan to produce safety belts in the near future. These belts are designed for workers who work at heights and on scaffolds. However, we will not mass-produce this product until it has passed all safety tests multiple times. Sometimes, I personally test the safety products to ensure their reliability. Our highest goal at Yahya Factory is to protect workers' lives. This is the right of every worker, whether they work in mines or weld on tall buildings, to feel safe and comfortable in their protective clothing and equipment.

My Management Techniques

Just as we watch war or sci-fi movies and don't take them too seriously, I believe we shouldn't take life's ups and downs too seriously either. Therefore, every morning, I remind myself, "The less greed one has, the more successful they will be."

In one of the verses of the Quran, the Merciful God says, "Whoever aligns their inner self with God's will (i.e., does not oppress and practices good deeds), all the particles of the universe align with them." This means God increases this person's knowledge and places the right people in their path.

I believe that a person's essence should be beautiful. Every morning when I wake up, I say to God, "God, show me who I should help today and where I can support someone in need." Let's not forget that blessings are not just about money. Blessings lie in security, honor, health, and peace. Being among good people and moving forward under God's command is beautiful.

The Ups and Downs of Entrepreneurship in Iran

To those who want to enter this field, the first truth I present, beyond all challenges, is that in Iran, there is no support for entrepreneurs, or it is extremely difficult to obtain. Even during the production of masks—a jihadist effort aimed at serving people and preventing the spread of COVID-19—the Vice President, the Minister of Industry, the Governor, and other officials only visited us to offer congratulations and make requests. Yet, throughout the production stages, we received no material or spiritual support. Thus, I say to anyone wanting to innovate in Iran: expect no help. You must have strong financial management. When you put your credit and capital on the line, you must have great perseverance. Sacrifice and humility are essential in this path. An Iranian entrepreneur must work until midnight and overcome countless obstacles. They must compensate for the shortcomings of the current politicians.

Anyone who wants to be an entrepreneur must first have confidence in themselves and their abilities in their field. They must show great dedication. Like an athlete who does not participate in the Olympics until they are sure of their capabilities, an entrepreneur must not give up halfway. They must stand firm against all adversities and bad faith, enduring everything. If they falter and give up, they not only risk their own life but also jeopardize the lives of the employees who stayed by their side with hope and aspiration. An entrepreneur must think more about the benefit of those around them than their own. Ultimately, the reward for an entrepreneur is an increase in their assets, but their effort and perseverance must surpass others. I always tell my family and friends, "The difference between us and Bill Gates is the number of zeros in our bank accounts. He has a few more zeros than us, that's all!"

A model entrepreneur should value every second of their life and not waste a moment of their productive working hours. By roughly calculating and deducting hours of sleep, traffic, and internet browsing from my remaining productive years, I realized that in the next twenty years, I only have about two and a half years of productive work time. Life is short, and we must move forward since there's no going back.

Advice to the Youth

To the young people and all those reading this book, I advise you first to be honest with yourselves. Know what you want from life and why you are on this path.

To determine if you can be an entrepreneur in the future, look at your abilities and aspirations. If money is important to you, choose a university major or job that is lucrative. Historically, not everyone has lived the same way or followed the same path. Even if we look at the lives of early humans and examine the details of cave dwellers' lives, we see that not everyone in the tribe was a hunter. A few went hunting, while some painted or engraved on the cave walls.

By looking at Maslow's hierarchy of needs, we can understand that today's entrepreneur, like those tribe members who left the safety of the cave to hunt, must increase their risk-taking ability. The first necessity for change is dissatisfaction with the current situation. When you are dissatisfied, you start changing or making changes. A small change over time leads to improvement, but a significant change after a while leads to transformation. A series of transformations lead to a leap. You need ten transformations in your life to make a leap. For instance, if a shopkeeper has few customers, merely cleaning the entrance won't create a transformation; it will only improve their situation slightly. However, if they change the shop's window display and decor and expand their advertising, they can witness a transformation and leap in their business.

In whatever you do, aim to be the best. Trust in God's will and do not wrong others. God Himself will handle your affairs and open miraculous paths for you.

Be the best in whatever task you undertake. Whether small or large, be trustworthy in small tasks, and God will deem you worthy of greater responsibilities and entrust you with them. Willpower is crucial in work. No two people on earth are alike. As an entrepreneur, you need strong knowledge of anthropology and behavior studies. If we cannot be successful entrepreneurs, the universe itself will not allow us to progress on this path. God's work is serious, and there is no room for trial and error in His kingdom. God does not tolerate anyone hindering His provision for His servants due to an entrepreneur's mistake. That's why I always say; a smart entrepreneur can use their good deeds for others as a shield. By doing good deeds, they can protect themselves from life's adversities. This principle is explicitly mentioned in the Quran. In verse 199 of Surah Al-Baqarah, God says: "Do good and do not cast yourselves into destruction with your own hands." This suggests that if you are destined for harm, you can avert it by doing good.

A model entrepreneur should avoid selfishness and arrogance and not let pride take over. They should personally train their staff several times a day and always stay in touch with them. The greater their position and reputation, the more humbly they should walk on the earth. If they own a luxury car, a lavish house, a yacht, or a private island, they should not flaunt their wealth before others. Because, in any situation, a person needs security and peace before wealth.

Final Words

In entrepreneurship, making money and accumulating wealth is very sweet, but sweeter still is the honor and glory that God bestows, making you dear and respected in the eyes of others. Therefore, be faithful to what is in your hands today and let God's blessings flow in your life and those around you with your good intentions. Trust in God's work in your life and do not fear taking risks with faith. In these times of fear and doubt, God has chosen you as an extraordinary entrepreneur to manifest His mighty miracles in your life and others.

The Analysis of Success Factors in
Yahya's Shoes

This quote must be from Henry David Thoreau, the famous American philosopher and writer, who once said, "I know of no more encouraging fact than the unquestionable ability of man to elevate his life by conscious endeavor." Thoreau was right; the strongest lever for change in a person's life is the power of their will.

From the Power of Will to the Power of Mind
Before the power of will, there is something called the power of the mind. It is actually the mind that dictates whether one can essentially use the power of will or not. If the mind is convinced that one can and should use the power of will, then we face a strong, effective willpower. This is why the literature on the principles of success in the world starts with mindset and self-awareness. There are often knots and brakes in the mind that prevent the release of our personal development and progress. If these mental brakes are not released, no amount of

effort will lead us anywhere. This is why advisors and experts in this field first work to untangle these knots and release these brakes so that a person's willpower and determination can operate at high speed.

Escaping Conditioned Minds

For a long time, the human mind was conditioned to believe that it couldn't change its current state. As Dr. Stephen Covey explains in his book "The 7 Habits of Highly Effective People"—which has been translated into Persian under various titles—people often find themselves in a triad of determinism:

1. Genetic Determinism: This is the belief that whatever we are is a result of our genetics. If, for example, we are angry or lazy, these traits have roots in the characteristics of our ancestors that have been passed down through our genes.

2. Psychic Determinism: This belief holds that our psychological makeup is largely shaped by our early life experiences. For instance, if something traumatic happened in childhood, its psychological consequences will manifest in adulthood and beyond.

3. Environmental Determinism: This suggests that our environment dictates who we are and what we can do, influenced by the pressures and messages from our surroundings.

But what is the result of these three types of determinism? It leads to the belief that we are not at fault and, as Dr. Covey puts it, we essentially cannot be proactive and are mostly reactive. All of this occurs in the mind. The mind tells us that we are trapped in determinism and not at fault, so any effort is futile. However, through human experience, these mental knots have been untangled one by one, unleashing the vast power of willpower both individually and collectively, leading to significant individual and collective achievements.

Sparks of Greatness

The literature on the principles of success has been established to prove that we possess an incredible power of will and that the first step is to resolve the mental blocks, then proceed with determination. Part of this understanding comes from studying the lives of those who have embodied this principle—starting from nothing and achieving significant success despite the triad of determinism. This has resulted in the rise of self-made millionaires in today's world, as noted by Brian Tracy. They have realized that mental and abstract success is achievable, that willpower is at their disposal, and that the necessary principles are available. Consequently, the number of successful self-made individuals is rapidly increasing.

A Real Experience

The life story of Yousef Sadeghi has been documented in a book produced in Iran. His life and childhood were devoid of any hope or brilliance, but he eventually became recognized as a national entrepreneur and one of Iran's leading business figures. Reviewing such biographies helps us understand that these achievements are possible, repeatable, and can be categorized and shared with others.

Passion for Work

Everyone in the world has a passion for something—music, singing, sports, football, running, performing, speaking, poetry, or solving complex mathematical problems. It becomes apparent that each person has a natural affinity for something, as if it was planted within them. In his book "The Power of Optimism," Price Pritchett talks about reaching your point of unique abilities, where you engage in work that you find easy to do and learn, to the extent that you don't realize you are doing something special because it feels natural. It is only when you realize that few others in your family, friends, or community can do what you do that you understand the uniqueness of your abilities.

Work Enthusiasts

Some people are passionate about their work. Surprised? I understand your astonishment, as we often have a particular aversion to work and effort, associating it with hardship and obligation. Usually, we do not choose our work or align it with our special abilities, leading to a joyless experience. However, when we engage in work we love, it brings endless joy. Arnold Schwarzenegger once said that only five percent of people can turn their hobbies into a beloved business, enjoying their lives rather than working. Kim Woo Choong, the founder of Daewoo, also discusses his extreme passion for work in his book "Every

Street is Paved with Gold," which we will briefly review:

• I have a great love for work. Many call me a workhorse because they think I find no pleasure in life and am a slave to work, doing whatever is demanded of me.

• This perception is incorrect. Why do you go on vacations, travel, or go to the seaside? Correct, to enjoy yourself. If I told you that the pleasure, I derive from completing a project is far greater than the enjoyment you get from travel, relaxation, and staying in luxurious hotels, wouldn't you say I am also engaging in leisure?

• I am astonished by young people wasting their time and energy in clubs. Don't they have a better place to exert their effort? Why not invest this energy in work?

• I am so obsessed with work that I sometimes forget my own birthday and even those of my wife and children. Fortunately, they are very understanding and I am deeply grateful to them.

• In whatever field you are, you should work so intensely that people label you. For example, "This student is a bookworm" or "This entrepreneur is a workhorse." When you get such labels, it means you are on the right path and deeply engaged in your work.

• Many believe that such extreme dedication to work harms family life. I believe that what damages family life is immorality, not a passion for work. When a Western entrepreneur divorces his wife at fifty and marries a younger woman he met on a European trip, that harms family life, not working hard. Eastern entrepreneurs have more moral commitment and thus

fewer family issues.
• Experience has taught me that a busy life leads to greater happiness, something I have observed in senior managers.
• I love my work so much that I have even abandoned simple leisure activities because work gives me everything I need.
• Note that this extreme passion for work is beneficial only if you love your work. If you view work as a tedious obligation, it will mentally drain you. To truly benefit from this passion, you must have a strong enthusiasm for your work and derive pleasure from it.

The Habit of Entrepreneurs

This intense passion for work is commonly observed among most entrepreneurs. When they face a problem, they sometimes spend several days at their workplace, not even going home, and sleeping there. They resemble athletes who, during the final days before a major competition, are deeply engaged in rigorous training to achieve their desired outcomes. Entrepreneurs are the same. They start by knowing they love their work. Then, they understand that the pleasure they derive from work matches the enjoyment others get from travel, socializing, sports, and dining out. Finally, they know that to achieve new successes, they must work hard to overcome inertia and get their systems and structures moving. This dedication to work results in numerous successes. As Mark Zuckerberg, the founder of Facebook, suggests, such passion can even circumvent many necessities, leading you to success through a shortcut. You might find yourself achieving your goals without the need for a detailed business plan or roadmap because this passion guides you step by step to your destination.

Justifying a Pleasant Imbalance

For many, understanding this concept might be difficult, and they might see it as an imbalance. However, this perception may not be accurate. When does an imbalance occur? It happens when you impose something on yourself beyond your capacity. But if what you impose on yourself aligns easily with your abilities and temperament and is supported and praised by others, then there is no imbalance. Consider the individual's level and characteristics. For example, three hours of daily physical training might seem excessive for you, but for a martial artist with a black belt, it's normal, and for a 5th-dan black belt holder, it's inadequate. Therefore, it's crucial to consider the context and level of individuals when discussing these matters.

A Real-Life Experience

Yusuf Sadeghi provides interesting insights into his passion for work. This passion was inherited from his father, or perhaps it was in their genes. Imagine, his father was so passionate about his work that he arrived a few hours late to his own wedding because he was looking for work boots! For others, this extreme passion for work might be hard to digest, but for people like Yusuf Sadeghi, who are deeply committed to work and entrepreneurship, it's completely normal. For them, work and entrepreneurship are not just specific duties at specific times; they are a way of life. They wake up with it, live with it, and go to bed with it. Therefore, it doesn't create an imbalance in their lives; it works well for them. Some personalities are inherently intense and need to focus intensely on something; otherwise, their busy minds might lead them astray.

Grant Cardone, a renowned entrepreneur, salesman, and global personal and economic development advisor, mentions that he earned nearly $800 million through sales. But how did someone who was once struggling with addiction and unemployment achieve such success? Simple: He achieved a deep self-awareness and realized that he had an intense personality, so he needed to keep himself engaged. Previously, addiction served this purpose, but he decided to focus on sales, work, and creating new businesses. The result? He became someone who created the 10X Rule for success and eventually became one of the most successful figures in his field, known to everyone. Yes, an intense passion for work has worked well for these individuals because their personalities are perfectly suited for entrepreneurship.

A Lesson from the Greatest Investor

Are you familiar with Warren Buffett? Most of you know this giant of the investment world. He is considered the greatest investor in history and spent years at the top of the world's wealthiest individuals list, often in the top ten. Due to his extensive studies, he offers numerous insights into financial and economic success, attracting a wide audience. But how did he reach a status that even the wealthiest individuals can only dream of? One of his notable quotes is: "I always knew I was going to be rich, and I never doubted it for a minute."

Lessons from a Successful Salesman

The key point we want to emphasize here is the certainty about the goal or event that will happen. Let's refer to some sayings by Doug Wead, one of the world's top sales advisors, to complete our discussion. He addresses the issue of doubt, which is a significant concern for salespeople worldwide. Salespeople face doubt every morning, noon, night, and even in their dreams. Therefore, Doug Wead tackles this issue, stating:

• Nothing exhausts and distresses a person's psyche more than self-doubt.
• Nothing undermines the impact of your words and actions like doubt.
• Nothing depletes your emotional fuel faster than doubt.

The Power of Certainty

Have you ever observed wildlife? Facing wild animals is often challenging and mostly impossible. For example, have you ever considered facing a lion, leopard, tiger, or even a hungry wolf? It's practically impossible. One reason is their inherent strength. Another reason is that when wild animals decide to do something, they have no doubt and their entire being is focused on the task. You might remember Mehran Modiri's quote in the movie "Wooden Bridge" where he talks about encountering lions in Africa, captivating his audience with his stories. The host asks him what he felt, but Modiri doesn't respond until after the event. He then explains that the grandeur of the lion lies in its absolute certainty and commitment to its desires, which is a source of its power.

This concept applies to humans as well. Human actions manifest through the power of will, which stems from mental strength. A unified mind leads to a strong will, whereas doubt fragments the mind and subsequently the will, resulting in fragmented actions and behaviors. As Kim Woo-Choong suggests, fragmented actions won't lead to success.

Never a Moment of Doubt

Warren Buffett says he always knew he would be rich and never doubted it for a moment. This story applies to many athletes and successful people worldwide. They train and work with such intensity as if there is no possibility of failure, not even a one percent chance. As the famous football player and coach Johan Cruyff said, when they are afraid, they attack harder and more fiercely. This certainty attracts success toward you.

Lessons from Alexander Graham Bell

Let's end with a few quotes from Alexander Graham Bell, the great inventor, to simplify our discussion. He says, "I cannot describe this power, this magic. I just know it exists and works. It works when you know exactly what you need to do and you don't stop until you achieve your goal." He also states, "Concentrate all your thoughts and efforts on the work at hand. The sun's rays do not burn until brought to a focus."

Imagine your mind as a sun emitting various rays. Each thought can be a ray telling you what to do or not to do. If these rays are scattered in different directions, your mental sun will be weak and dim, lacking brightness and intensity. But if all these rays focus on one task, goal, or concern, it's like placing a magnifying glass in your mind, concentrating all these rays in one spot. Naturally, the resulting effect will be powerful and impactful, won't it?

What Does the Law of Attraction Say?

On the other hand, perhaps this principle can be explained by the Law of Attraction. Now, you may either believe in such a concept or not. We assume that you don't believe in this law. However, as a human being, you interact with your environment and with others. Similarly, others interact with you, and these interactions lead to mental and psychological exchanges. In these relationships, you are influenced by others and your surroundings, just as they are influenced by you. Essentially, there is an exchange of energy. In these interactions, you attract certain things, and others attract certain things from you. You convey messages to others, such as: "I am serious," "I am confident," "I am completely certain of my success," and "I have no doubt that my goals will be achieved." When others receive these messages, they reflect them back to you, offering you opportunities and successes, both big and small.

Imagine for a moment that you are a senior manager, CEO, or president of an organization looking for someone to manage the positions and roles you have in mind. To whom would you offer these opportunities? Most jobs are not given to applicants but to those who pursue their work and goals with great seriousness and certainty, without any doubts. These qualities make others admire them and want to provide them with golden opportunities. In fact, if they sought these positions themselves, they might not have achieved such results. This can be seen as an interpretation of a mind without doubt and the power of will, which may not be entirely dissimilar to the Law of Attraction.

A Real-Life Experience

When we review the life of Yousef Sedighi, we see that his complete confidence in his abilities existed from the early years of his youth. He knew that whatever he undertook, he would succeed. This is akin to Brian Tracy's advice to plan, work, and set goals as if failure does not exist. Sedighi exemplifies those who act as if there is no failure in their world and believe they can achieve whatever they desire. You might think such an idea is unrealistic since everyone fails at some point. Yes, the final result might not be in our hands, but being undoubted in our goals, actions, and plans makes us psychologically calmer and significantly increases our chances of success.

It's natural that not all professional athletes win gold medals and first places, but the point is that maintaining unity in mind, action, will, and planning will not harm us and might even lead to outstanding successes. Just look at Yousef Sedighi to understand what we mean; a man who from his youth uprooted and discarded any doubt in his abilities, acting as if failure did not exist in his world, knowing he would achieve whatever he intended.

If you have read Brian Tracy's books, one point is heavily emphasized. Tracy begins by telling his own story; what his situation was, where he started from, and where he ended up. After years of manual labor, working on ships, and selling, he wasn't making progress in sales until he discovered the biggest and most important question of his life: Why were the successful salespeople in his company successful, and what principles and techniques did they use?

A Simple Yet Great Solution

Brian quickly asked these successful salespeople about the reasons for their success. They eagerly shared their tips with him. Being a good listener, Brian started implementing these techniques. In his sales process, he tried to follow the learned rules for talking, closing deals, presenting, handling objections, pricing, and so on. Gradually, his sales increased. Surprised, he sought out successful salespeople from other companies, learned their techniques, and his sales grew again. Seeing how well this approach worked, he read books on the subject, understood their points, and implemented them. When he saw this method working well, he attended seminars and consultations on the topic, applying what he learned. His sales grew more and more until he became the top salesperson in his company. Eventually, he was given a larger office with dozens of staff, effectively becoming the second-in-command. Later, he joined competing companies with a much higher salary.

Learning from the Best

Brian Tracy emphasizes learning and working scientifically in his teachings. He adheres strictly to this principle. He still expresses amazement at how simple and effective success can be and how distant others are from it. Yes, he is still amazed by this simple and powerful rule: observe what the best in your field do, replicate it, get feedback, refine, and continue.

The Deepest Layer of Knowledge

In a saying attributed to Imam Ali (AS), it is stated that the shallowest level of knowledge is that which merely flows from your tongue, while the deepest level is that which manifests in your actions and behavior. If we use this saying as our criterion, we realize how simple the principles of success are, provided we strive to achieve the highest levels of it, namely, acting upon it. Dr. Ali Shah Hosseini, a national entrepreneur and entrepreneurship instructor, offers an interesting point in this regard. He notes, "If a specialist or consultant whom I trust tells me to go to a certain place at a specific time and throw a certain number of small stones into a particular well or river, I would certainly do it without asking why, because I know there must be wisdom in it, and this approach has led me to good places."

Scientific Work in Business

This approach is also the beginning of working scientifically in business. Business is closely related to gaining experience, but remember that wisdom consists of the cumulative experiences of ourselves and others. If others have followed our experiences and achieved success, why should we focus only on our own experiences? Instead, we can learn from their educational points and implement them.

One of the best ways to do this is through the apprenticeship system, which Yousef Sedighi also mentions in his biography. Interested in work, he started as an apprentice, learning the ins and outs and principles of the job to apply them. Even when he launched his first production line and factory at the age of 24, he proceeded this way. Initially, he apprenticed to learn everything, and when he realized he could produce a certain boot or safety shoe, he started working. He admits he should have focused more, but he started immediately. Later, to advance scientifically, he added a lot of business knowledge and training to his skills.

Points from Rolf Dobelli

Now, regarding the importance of acting quickly and adding necessary points to oneself, let's consider insights from Rolf Dobelli, the author of reputable books on personal development. He says:

- The best ideas come to you when you are writing, not when you are thinking. Next time you need to make an important decision, think about it carefully, but only up to the point of maximum reflection.
- A friend wanted to start a pharmaceutical company. He spent ten years preparing, studying hundreds of entrepreneurship books, learning how to market his products, reviewing extensive market research, and drafting dozens of business plans. The result? Nothing yet. He always reaches a point where his thoughts tell him, "It's a good idea, but it depends on your execution and the actions of your competitors."
- The best ideas come when you are writing, not thinking. When thinking about a subject, you reach a point where no matter how much you think, you won't advance even a millimeter. From this moment on, the additional information gained from thinking about that subject becomes zero. This is called the "point of maximum reflection."
- If reflection is a pocket flashlight, acting is like a real spotlight.
- Why do we tend to overthink issues far beyond the point of maximum reflection? Because it's easier. It's much simpler to think about issues than to take the initiative to act on them. Speculation is more enjoyable than action. As long as you are weighing your options, the risk of failure is zero, but once you act, the risk of failure increases significantly. That's why people prefer thinking and analyzing over taking action.
- Picasso said that to know what you want to draw; you must start drawing. It's the same with your life; to know what you

want; you must start acting. This idea might give you a push, but be aware that merely thinking about a good life won't lead you to it.

• Next time you need to make an important decision, think carefully, but only up to the point of maximum reflection. You'll be surprised at how quickly you reach this point. Once you do, turn off your flashlight and turn on the spotlight. This method works both at work and home, whether you are investing in your career or seeking to improve your romantic life.

The Right Way to Learn

These are interesting points. This doesn't mean not studying or working scientifically, nor does it mean avoiding consultation. But these things have their time and place. Beyond a certain point, you must act, which is what people like Yousef Sedighi excel at. Even if you have limited knowledge but high action power and quick response, you will still succeed. The more persistent and hardworking you are, the more you can learn.

Let's share a story from the book "Gurdjieff's Masters." In this book, one of Gurdjieff's students, a great Sufi master of the last hundred years, searches for his teachers to see who they were. In this process, he realizes that what's important are Gurdjieff's teachings, not Gurdjieff himself. He reads about his path and teachings that led him to greatness. In an encounter with one of Gurdjieff's teachers, Sheikh Abdullah Shater, he reads: "... If I don't ask questions, how do I learn? The Sheikh replied: Pay attention to your question; learning and asking questions are two different things. You learn by doing, not by asking questions. It's not about why you should read a particular book or when and where you should read it; you need to read the book to experience its content and act. You feel the need to ask questions. You believe it's your right to ask questions, and you think you have enough intelligence and wisdom to understand the answers. You likely have a higher education and a university degree. But does your "intelligence and wisdom" alone help you in the field of handicrafts if you lack skill and experience in that area? Do skin diseases heal faster just because you have a university degree? Can you run faster than a well-trained but uneducated runner simply because you are much smarter? Does your intelligence make your legs grow wings? Education, intelligence, and knowledge are only beneficial if you can apply them correctly and in the right context.

Yes, this is the approach that people like Yousef Sedighi have adhered to: start quickly and learn what you need along the way, just like a sponge absorbing water and getting heavier. They are sponges for the necessary points and absorb everything they need during the journey. Ultimately, it's an interesting method; you start quickly without wasting time and absorb the necessary points as you go.

One of the crucial discussions in the field of business development is about learning and having a strong desire to learn. Many businesses start well and progress successfully but falter halfway simply because they lose the desire to learn. This lack of interest in learning arises from the fact that your burning enthusiasm for learning elevates you to a level of expertise where you stand head and shoulders above others. You then get caught in a sense of pride in your business and might assume that things will always remain the same. However, others are learning intensely and advancing, and on the highway of competition, if you move at a normal speed, many will overtake you. This false pride causes many to stagnate and face failure.

Aggressive Learning and Attitude

Brian Tracy, in his books, including "Principles of Victory Based on Military Techniques," mentions the process of aggressive behavior in business. He cites examples of successful military operations where victory was solely due to an aggressive spirit and a drive to move forward. Tracy applies this idea to aggressive marketing and sales, connecting the two. Interestingly, in aggressive marketing, one of the techniques is specialization. If you have expertise, you practically push others aside and move forward. Specialization, along with creativity and other factors, keeps you in an aggressive stance toward your target market, leading to greater success. Naturally, no one can easily compete with an individual, group, or business whose advantage is their expertise, which they continue to develop daily.

Whether you are in an individual position or managing a business, you must understand that education and learning are even more crucial than daily bread. These teachings and learnings will ensure more security, income, respect, and influence in your surroundings and the market and among your target groups. For this learning process, you must have a consistent and ongoing program. You should not think that if you have reached a certain level of knowledge and expertise, it is enough. Yousef Sedighi mentions the learning and training system in American and Japanese businesses. They start teaching their employees up to a certain level, but he notes that in the Japanese business system, this level is much higher, as they do not stop at a certain level of learning. As Sedighi says, they train their employees to the point where they can understand from the sound of the machines whether they are working well or if there is a problem and where the issue lies.

A Real Experience

Yousef Sedighi emphasizes the importance of professional and relevant knowledge and learning in today's world and developed countries. He points out that this is why teachers' salaries in these countries are the highest and they are the most respected. He is not just referring to school teachers but to those who fundamentally teach the professional principles of a job and profession. According to him, they do not abandon education, ensuring that employees reach the highest level of expertise. This way, any business can exhibit aggressive behavior in its market and competitive field, reaching the best positions. Sedighi mentions that their business employs two thousand workers, and they proceed with this method, never wasting time or getting sidetracked, working intensively to keep the business at its peak. They understand that the peak of the business is also their peak and economic security.

Choosing the Right Paths

When you are walking through city streets or even riding your bike or motorcycle, your speed is limited, no matter how much you desire speed and progress. To go faster, you need to get to the streets. If you want even more speed and reach your destination quicker, you must get to the highway. However, you will still have a speed limit and cannot drive infinitely fast. The main point is that every path you take has its own speed limit, and beyond that, it won't allow you to move forward.

Time Limits for Employee Work

The same situation applies to economic development and business growth. As long as you are engaged in employee work, your progress will be limited. How much income do you expect? Both your hours and your physical and mental capacities are limited. Therefore, no matter how focused, efficient, and fast you work, there is a limit beyond which you cannot progress. This is the problem with being an employee or worker for others; your progress ceiling is limited. This limitation might not be an issue for some, as they might be content with this level and have defined their lives accordingly. However, those aiming for the most economic development must inevitably think about other paths to economic growth. Therefore, every path you take depends significantly on your ultimate goal.

The Famous Financial Independence Quadrant

Here, it is useful to refer to Robert Kiyosaki's famous quadrant from his books. In his well-known books, often centered around financial intelligence and independence, Kiyosaki explains that you have a quadrant divided into four equal parts: two on the left and two on the right. On the left, you deal with employee and self-employment positions, jobs requiring your personal time for income. Even if you earn high incomes, this income flow will stop once you stop working. This contradicts the definition of financial independence. Financial independence is defined as how long you can maintain your current quality of life without working. Naturally, employees and workers might only last a couple of months. Some might have more savings and last a year or two. However, when it comes to selling your car and spending personal assets, financial independence has ended. Ultimately, financial independence is closely related to time: how long you can continue your current lifestyle without working. Some can last a month, others several months or years, and some can maintain it indefinitely, reaching financial retirement and comfortably quitting their jobs, although they rarely do so because their work motivation changes to other goals.

Investment and Business Management Quadrants

In the right quadrants of the financial independence square, we have business management and investment jobs. You either create a production line or a production structure for yourself, which can operate without your presence because everyone knows their job. You can travel and return a year later to find the factory working profitably. In the investment quadrant, you invest your money in places that yield the highest returns without needing your presence. This way, an income stream is created without your direct involvement. Since there are no limits, you can experience significant growth, sometimes even hundreds or thousands of times more in the case of startups, leading to incomes and assets previously unimaginable in just a few years.

Quotes from Robert Kiyosaki

Let's review some quotes from Robert Kiyosaki: "Each of us falls into one of the four quadrants of the cash flow quadrant. Where our cash flow comes from determines our place. Many of us rely on monthly paychecks and thus remain employees. Another group is self-employed. Employees and self-employed individuals fall on the left side of the cash flow quadrant. The right side is for those who earn from businesses they own or investments they make. The cash flow quadrant is about four different groups of people who form the business world, each unique in their position. This chart helps you recognize your current position and where you want to be in the future, identifying the path to financial independence. Although financial independence can be achieved in all four quadrants, the skills of a business owner or investor will help you reach your financial goals faster. A successful employee must also succeed in the investment quadrant."

Don't Succumb to Your Fears
The main issue is, as Brian Tracy says, you can achieve financial independence even with employee and self-employment jobs. By increasing your productivity and focusing intensely in the first few years, you can grow and then invest the income. It's not that employee and worker jobs are inherently flawed; however, even with these jobs, you must consider savings and the right quadrants, which are investment and business ownership. Another significant point is that many people lack the interest or courage for investment or business ownership due to the comfort of salaried jobs. This negative addiction to working and receiving a fixed monthly salary gradually conditions you, making you reluctant to try new ventures. According to the law of compound effect, after several years, this habit becomes so ingrained that it immobilizes you, making it hard to break the pattern. Starting a business or investment requires a lot of knowledge, and the risk of failure is high, deterring many from participating. This is why financial independence remains limited; it all stems from our fears and bad habits.

Cultivating an Entrepreneurial and Investment Spirit
Yousef Sedighi established his factory at the age of twenty-four, an age when many young people are graduating and still figuring out what to do. He, engaged in buying, selling, and importing safety shoes, identified opportunities well. Realizing that the quality of the shoes he traded was inadequate and there was no production line in Iran, he decided to produce these shoes him-

self. Despite lacking specific experience in starting a business, he boldly entered the field, learning necessary points along the way. Later, he chose to enhance his knowledge to work scientifically and systematically. However, he did not succumb to the negative addiction most people surrender to, having a steady job with a fixed monthly income. Such addiction gradually kills the courage to take action, turning a person into an average individual. This is a path many of us need to take, even if it involves the risk of failure. Interestingly, in Islamic culture, wage work is discouraged, not implying idleness but favoring industries, trade, and commerce, which create economic fluidity and cash flow in society. It is narrated that if a Muslim has a break during a war, it is commendable to engage in trade. Such attitudes lead individuals toward financial independence, keeping their entrepreneurial spirit alive and sharpening it.

Business: A World of Calculations

The business world has a significant relationship with mathematics and calculations. Sun Tzu, a great military strategist who emerged in China 2,500 years ago, was also a military commander whose military principles are still taught in major military and even non-military universities worldwide. In one section of his book "The Art of War," he mentions that victory in a war result.

From Illusion to Reality

Yousef Sedighi has a great interest in mathematics. He is deeply invested in the precision and exactness of math. Not only does he think carefully, but he also seeks advice from others to ensure that his information, whether internal or external and business-related, aligns closely with facts and is not based on guesses, illusions, or similar things. He understands well that our successes are based on our assumptions, and if our assumptions are wrong, our successes will be destroyed. This is why he calculates intensively and tries to extract his successes from these numerous calculations. This strong realism of his moves him away from illusions and towards the kind of realism that is preferred and needed in the job market—a practice that all entrepreneurs should pay close attention to.

On the Path of Quality

It is a natural behavior among all people to desire the best and highest quality services and products at the fastest possible time, in the simplest and most respectful manner, and at the lowest or most reasonable price. Brian Tracy, in one of his books, describes this as the essence of economic science: people prefer quicker profits to delayed ones, higher profits to lower ones, more certain profits to less certain ones, and so on. When you have the necessary quality, you are precisely in the spotlight. Without needing any special advertising or marketing, you will easily dominate the market. In fact, it is the people who will promote and advertise your product and services by word of mouth, and what could be better than that? In the science of branding, there is an important point: if you understand it well, you can shine in the business world. This teaching states that every definition others make of you and your product or service is as impactful as dozens or hundreds of advertisements that you and your organization carry out. In fact, people pay more attention to recommendations from their friends, relatives, and trusted individuals than to advertisements. In this domain, suitable quality can lead to you being repeatedly emphasized and even recommended by others, and what could be better for your business than such an occurrence?

From Quality to Quality Control

Businesses that want to have high quality must also have high quality control. Simply wanting and claiming that quality should grow does not lead to growth. To achieve this, you need to design a structure and system for it. In management, what you expect does not happen; what you demand and hold your personnel and structure accountable for does. For this purpose, you need a quality control structure so that instead of your product or service being returned from the market, it is the customer who returns. If you do not design such a structure, it will be your product and service that comes back, and you will go bankrupt.
Forty People for Quality Control!
Sedighi mentions that in his factories, he sometimes employs forty people in the quality control department to extract the best possible quality. Forty people for quality control is a very high number; it might even be possible to start another production line with this workforce. However, he understands well that an-

yone can usually produce bad products and services, but it is the good products and services that not everyone can produce, and this is what the market is hungry for. Once, engineer Soltani, a reputable entrepreneur in the field of game-making and children's games production, mentioned that he once went to the market and came back. When he returned to his company, he told his employees to work with peace of mind and not to worry because the competitors, sellers, and stores he saw—who were considered competitors—were behaving so primitively and poorly with customers that with our level of quality, we would remain at the top for a long time, and no one would come close to us.

In the Iranian business context, it is common for most businesses to pay little attention to customers and how they treat them, losing many opportunities as a result. Now, if a business focuses intensely on the quality of its work and makes quality its main concern, it will achieve brilliant successes and strengthen its position. In this regard, both the concern for quality and the establishment of structures to ensure it will be highly effective—something that most businesses might abandon due to its costs, but which people like Yousef Sedighi not only have not abandoned but have pursued with great determination.

Iranian Great Entrepreneurs

A 1000 set of Iranian Great Entrepreneurs

Dr. Reza Yadegari
Mahshid Sanaeefard

The Winners of the Prestigious
Jalal Al-e Ahmad Literary Award

To access Great Entrepreneurs Series

www.ingramcontent.com/pod-product-compliance
Lightning Source LLC
Chambersburg PA
CBHW052206070526
44585CB00017B/2091